FULFILLED

The ABC's of a Great Life

Wendy Treat

Table of Contents

My Personal Testimony of Victory

In this book, I would like to share with you the key principles that can help you live as a fulfilled woman of God. But first, I'd like to relate a testimony from my life that exemplifies the gut-level decisions we must all make to live out these principles. I had to put many of these principles into action during the course of the circumstance I am about to describe.

My husband, Casey, and I ride bicycles regularly. Years ago, Casey rode his bike from Issaquah, Washington, to Wenatchee, Washington, with another brother from our church. The trip is approximately 140 miles and goes over two mountain passes. They rode their bikes while I followed along in the van and provided them with food and fresh water. My bicycle was in the van, so before they reached Wenatchee I jumped out and rode the last 30 miles with them.

A few days later, the thought occurred to me that I also wanted to ride from Issaquah to Wenatchee. When I told Casey, he asked if he could go with me. I told him he could come if he wanted to, but I wasn't doing it for him to come along. The ride was a goal that I really wanted the satisfaction of accomplishing

1

for myself. It was a natural, rather than spiritual vision and goal, but I needed to prove to myself that I could ride over both mountains and succeed at riding 140 miles in one day. Casey said he would come with me, and I agreed.

I had been riding my bike for about twelve years at this time but had not ridden outdoors for the past five years. I had been riding an indoor exercise bike consistently, averaging three to five miles per day, in addition to other types of exercises. Once I had set my goal, I realized I needed to pick up the pace. I knew I couldn't continue to ride three miles daily and expect to ride 140 miles with two mountain passes in one day. So, I started biking outside more and increased the miles I was riding.

With the days getting closer, I was becoming increasingly more excited. I had planned to make the ride on a particular weekend in May. I didn't want to go in June, July, or August because it would be too hot. Our schedule was very busy, so once I planned the day there were no free weekends for the next six weeks. I had to go on these particular days, wait until the middle of the hot weather, or wait until fall. I continued to train outside, putting in all the extra miles I could.

The next thing I knew, it was only two days before the ride! The sun was shining and it was beautiful. I thought, *Glory to God, the week looks good!*

The next day came and it started out gorgeous. Later that day, about 3:00 p.m., it started to sprinkle. By 4:00 p.m., it wasn't sprinkling; it was RAINING!

I was supposed to leave for the ride at 5:00 a.m. the next morning. I looked out my window. Trees were blowing and bending, and I became angrier by the minute, thinking, *No, it cannot rain! My goal and my vision are to get over the mountains, and I'm going tomorrow! I have to go tomorrow!*

Being a woman of faith, I went to bed early. I had everything ready for the next morning. I had my bananas (bike riders always eat bananas) and my sandwiches ready. My clothes were set out, and my alarm was set for 4:30 a.m.

Full of anticipation, I woke up at 4:20 a.m. You know you're excited about something when you wake up at that time without an alarm!

Casey said, "Do you see any sunlight out there?"

Black clouds were everywhere, but I could see in the center of one section and said, "Casey, look! There's some blue sky right over there."

He rolled over and practically went back to sleep, but I was out of bed and fired up. I finally said, "Get up!" Of course, he wanted to wait another hour to make sure we were really going to go.

Our friend was coming to take us to our starting point, so I said, "Get up! Doug is already committed to be here. Get up! Get up!"

"Ya, ya, ya," he said. I was sure he had thought, *She might give up so I'm not going to wake up too much.*

"Up now!"

Finally, he got up and wandered around.

"Get dressed. Come on, let's go!"

I ran downstairs and got breakfast. I was so excited! By the time our friend arrived, Casey was ready. We got in the van and drove down the road. I thought about our bikes, how they were all shined up and ready to go.

When we reached the place in Issaquah where we were going to start, it wasn't raining, but it was dark for 6:15 a.m., especially at that time of the year.

I said, "Okay, let's go."

Casey said, "Now, you're sure this is what you want to do, honey? It's not going to rain or anything?"

"Come on, let's go," I said. "We can't do it any other time, and it's not raining right now."

We got on our bikes and started on our way.

We had ridden about two miles when it started to rain. I always wear sunglasses so that dirt and bugs don't get in my eyes. With my dark sunglasses and the rain and dark clouds, it was difficult to see where I was going. The rain was really coming down, but so far neither of us had commented about it.

Casey began singing a song we sometimes sang at our church, "Be Bold, Be Strong" by Morris Chapman. He sang for a while and said, "It looks like we've got a testimony coming up!"

I laughed. "Honey, it's going to quit raining. No problem. Let's keep going."

We talked while continuing to pedal. And it kept raining.

Eventually, we had ridden about ten to 15 miles and were soaked by that time. We were also very cold. My hair hung down from under my helmet, and water was dripping all over my face. My gloves and jacket were soaked. Everything was drenched.

Approximately three hours after we had left, another friend planned to meet us in our van. We were going to eat lunch and change into shorts because it was to be sunny and hot.

Eventually, we rode into North Bend, and Casey said, "Honey, we had better call and tell her to come right now to give us dry clothes."

We stopped at a McDonalds, made our phone call, and ordered hot drinks. We decided to continue riding and have our friend meet us along the road. Unfortunately, it was still pouring as we began our climb up Snoqualmie Pass.

At the time we made the phone call, we had ridden about 40 miles. Casey's last words to our friend were, "Just remember we are freezing out here!" This person had never driven to

Wenatchee, so she didn't know exactly where she was going. However, we figured she would catch us within 15 miles or so. Soon we had ridden 50 miles. Then we hit 60 miles. We had already gone over the top of Snoqualmie Pass and were on our way down.

The enjoyment of going up a hill is going back down, but we were so cold and wet we didn't enjoy the ride down the hill! We were hanging on to our brakes just to make sure we were going slow enough that we didn't freeze.

I had laughed when we reached the top of Snoqualmie Pass because I looked over to the side of the road and realized that we were in snow. "You know, Casey, the reason we don't snow ski is because we hate getting cold. What are we doing up here?"

Soon we were going on 65 miles and coming into Cle Elum. At this point, I wasn't talking much anymore. I was at the place where nothing would help. Our sandwiches and bananas were gone; everything was gone. We were freezing, miserable, and hungry. My only thought was, *Where is that van?*

Casey said, "Honey, let's stop and get something to eat. There's a little cafe up ahead that is right on the main road."

Up to that point, we hadn't gone off the road. Casey left his bike on the side of the road so our friend would be sure to see it when she drove past.

We ordered hamburgers and sat there for a few minutes. When we were ready to go again, all of a sudden I looked out the window and saw our van drive by. Casey said the look on my face was incredible.

I yelled, "Casey, RUN! RUN! OH, NOOOOOO!"

Casey looked at me and thought he was going to have to carry me. We had only been in there for ten minutes, and now the van was gone. Gone! For some reason, I just knew when she drove by that she wasn't coming back. I knew she would not turn around. I just sat there and thought, *What am I going to do? What am I going to do now?*

My hands and fingers were beginning to move a little bit after sitting in the restaurant for those few minutes, and the shakes were just going away. I thought, *Okay, God, You know my vision and goal was to make it all the way. Well, I'm already wet. I might as well go for the rest of it.* I looked up at Casey and said, "Be BOLD! Be STRONG! For the LORD."

We got back on our bikes and were on our way again.

Casey said, "Maybe she'll come back."

"Casey, at this point, we're going to make it all the way." Something rose up within me, and I knew we were going to make it all the way. I was glad she did not see us because I was so cold I would have gotten in the van and given up my vision and my dream.

We rode until we finally came to the bottom of Bluett Pass, which was our second and final mountain pass. Right before we started up the mountain, we stopped at a little store and bought ourselves prizes for the top of the hill. Mine was a Snickers bar. We put our prizes in our back pockets and pedaled up the hill. We noticed then that it had stopped raining. In fact, we could even see blue sky. Remember how drenched we had been? But now, as we rode along, we dried out. My gloves, pants, jacket, feet—everything got warmer. My fingers could even move.

Soon, we were singing as we rode along. I knew there was one remaining part of the pass that was hard, but once we completed it, we would be at the top. I could see it coming.

I shifted to low gears and started pedaling. Soon, we were almost to the top.

Casey asked, "Do you want to eat your Snickers bar now?"

I said, "No, that's my prize for the top." I could hardly wait because I knew the rest of the trip was basically downhill.

When we reached the top, we ate our bars. We were feeling pretty good when guess who drove up?

Our friend had driven all the way to Wenatchee to my sister-in-law's house. When my sister-in-law realized our friend had missed us, she jumped in the van and drove to the top of Bluett Pass.

"Yay! I've come to get you." She thought she had saved the day.

I looked at her. "Are you kidding me? No way! You get back in the van, and we'll see you in Wenatchee."

"I can't believe you guys are so strange that you are going to go all the way down," she said.

I had 50 miles left to go and my vision would be complete. We finally convinced her we were serious, so she got back in the van and drove away.

Before I finish the story, let me show you a couple of principles. Number one, I had a vision and a goal I wanted to reach. You also have visions and goals that you want to reach. God has put a desire in your heart, something you want to accomplish. It may be physical, financial, social, or spiritual, but there's something rising up in you that you want to do. That's what happened to me with this bike ride. I wanted to do it. I wanted to accomplish it! But when the day came for me to actually meet that goal, it seemed like every demonic force came out fighting to take the victory away from me.

Do you realize that when you have a vision or goal, the devil will come to try to steal it from you? He will send every storm he can against you, whether it's people saying, "Oh, you can't do that. That's not a very good idea," or "It's just the natural circumstances of life that come up." I have talked with many people who have said, "I don't know how I keep getting better and better on my job. I never thought I would be able to accomplish this much." I just say, "Yeah, keep going for it!"

The devil will come to you and say, "You're not smart enough to reach that goal. You'll never be the president. You'll never be in charge. You'll never be in management. You'll never be a good parent, a good father, a good mother, a good husband, a good wife. You'll never make it. Just look at all these good reasons."

Then there are the storms of life that come against you that say, "Don't do it! Don't do it! Don't do it!"

The storms were raging the day I rode to Wenatchee. The storms said, "Don't do it!" When we were riding; when we called home for dry clothes; when we were sitting in the restaurant, the storms were on. I had already gotten through the first stage of the storm in the sense of going.

You may get going in your vision and goal, and it may not look good at first. You might be cold and miserable. You might be saying, "I don't know if I can do this!" And then, all of a sudden, the van comes driving by and someone says, "Come on in! You have done so well. You've done more than anyone else you know. It's really enough. You've given it such a good try."

In your job, you have been telling people about Jesus Christ. You've been putting yourself out there and they have been knocking you down. The devil will come and say, "Why should you go through all these problems? These people don't even care! Just give up! They aren't going to get saved anyway." Even a Christian brother or sister may say, "You've really been taking it. Why don't you just relax for a while?" They are saying to you, "Get in the van. Take it easy. You've done so much already. You don't have to go all the way."

That van is so tempting. I know that, in the natural, if our van had stopped, I would have been in it in a second. I would have run to get in. And that's why I thank God the van drove by. That was His mercy and grace saving me from defeat.

It's those times when we are so far down and can't see any light at the end of the tunnel that we need God's grace and mercy to help us out. There are times when we want to jump in and give up. There have been times I've been frustrated or mad. I've thought, *I just can't do it,* and that's when I've had to say, "I'm going to do it anyway."

In the poem "Footprints," a person asks, "Why is there only one set of footprints at this one place?" Jesus answered, "That's when I carried you. That's where I had to lift you up." The van driving by was when God's grace and mercy picked me up and moved me into a place of victory. I knew I had a choice. I knew I had a decision to make, so I said, "No, I'm going to do it now."

You have a choice. You can pick God's way or you can reject God's help. I know people who have done that. They have said, "I don't care," and they haven't gone the extra mile to move beyond the pain or the turmoil of the problems. Don't be one of the casualties.

You see, I had a choice, and I made the choice because I wanted to. I said, "Okay, praise God, let's go. Let's get on our bikes and go for it." When I made that decision to go for it, the rain quit coming down!

It's amazing that when we take another step, the storms become lighter. It's almost like the devil realizes he can't put the same stress on us anymore because we are prepared to stand up and fight. The devil wants to stop you before you actually run the whole race. He wants to deceive you into getting into the van too soon.

When my sister-in-law drove up, it would have been easy for me to get into the van. I could have said, "I did great. I've already made it through the storm. All I have left to do is ride down the mountain. That's downhill. Anybody can ride downhill."

But not everybody can ride downhill. Some people settle for good when God wants them to have the best! You've heard the statement, "Good is the enemy of best." Too many of us, in the renewing of our minds, have settled for good. Many of us have not pressed for the PERFECT will of God.

In your marriage, have you settled for just getting along? The kind of marriage God wants you to have is one where you look at your husband or wife and say, "Oh God, thank you! Thank you that you gave me this one!" I don't care if you have been married one year, five years, ten years, 20 years, or 100 years, you should look at your spouse and say, "Oh God, I have the best." Don't just slide by. Go for the BEST in your marriage.

This is also true of your job. Some of you have settled for, "I'm making enough money now to pay my bills," but you're not pressing for the BEST.

Some of you could do so much more in your ministry. You say, "I have a good life group." My question is, "How many new meetings have you started?" You say, "What do you mean, started? I'm doing good just to keep what I've got going." Get a vision. Set goals in your life to go for something. And then press on until you reach the top. Go for the GOLD!

Let me finish the story. My sister-in-law had come to rescue us, but we sent her back to Wenatchee in the van. We got back on our bikes and headed down that final hill. We had about 45 miles left of pretty basic, easy riding. Of course, after almost 100 miles of stooping over on the bicycle, your neck stiffens and your bottom gets sore, and you become tired of it. Even though I was over the worst part and on my way into home base, it was still rather tiring. It can still be a challenge, even downhill. I wanted to say, "Let's do something different." Reaching for the best can seem tedious. You can get discouraged and want to give up. That's when you have to say, "I won't give up."

We were riding, getting closer and closer to our goal. I saw landmarks along the way that told me I was getting closer and closer. Soon, we were at the point where I knew there was one last little hill. Every time I've driven to Wenatchee, I've thought, "That's a good-sized hill!" At that point, it seemed huge. But, it was amazing what happened, as if I had been out for a short five-mile ride. I stood up and went zip, right to the top! I was up that hill in no time at all.

That's another thing about God. When you're going along in your race and you have your vision and your hope, you also must have patience to endure to the end. Many times, you have to use your faith and your patience. Other times, when you're just starting off, a little hill like that could be a tremendous trial. But when you've already gone through the storms as I had, and you've made the commitment to go for it, you'll make it to the end. When I got to that hill, I just zipped to the top. I thought, *This is the way it is as you grow as a Christian.* At first, those hills are really hard and quitting can be tempting, but as you grow in God, you pop right over those hills.

When we rode into my brother's driveway and had reached our goal, all I could think was how I had been tempted not to win. You may be in a storm right now that you think is impossible to win.

I recently talked with a sister about her marriage. She told me, "I don't think you understand. I hate my husband!" I've talked to people in the financial distress of thousands of dollars of debt, and they've said, "I don't think you understand. There's no way out. We have to go bankrupt and just give up!" I told them, "Right now you are in a storm. It seems like every demon force that can muster up any strength is coming against you. But you have to recognize that God, in His mercy and grace, has given you principles from the Word that will cause you to win."

When you have a vision and a goal, you can say, "I'm going to reach that goal!" You can make a decision and then use your faith and patience to reach your goal.

Don't give up. Don't get into the van. Don't listen to the lies of the devil or other people. God has a better way for you. Use the principles in this book and you will have a victory in your life!

A

ATTITUDE

Romans 12:2

"And do not be conformed to this world, but be transformed by the renewing of your mind, that you may prove what *is* that good and acceptable and perfect will of God."

In order to be a fulfilled person, your thinking must be in line with God's Word. You must be willing to exchange your old way of thinking for God's way of thinking. Most thinking is habitual and comes from the way you have been trained to think about and respond to different situations.

As you are in the process of growing and changing, sometimes old thinking returns. You may wonder, *Why did I think that? That doesn't even fit me anymore!* You're right, it really doesn't fit you, but you have an old habit of thinking that way and it takes time to retrain yourself to think God's way. Whenever the "wrong" circumstance comes along, the old thought habit kicks into gear and your mind will go right into your old thought patterns.

For example, I had to renew my mind to believe that people liked me. At times when I was alone, I used to think, *I wonder if they really like me.* That was my old way of thinking. When I am with people now, I do not feel insecure as I used to. I no longer feel that people are thinking, *I wish she would get out of here. She is boring!*

The key is recognizing when the old way of thinking has kicked into gear. Tell yourself, "Wait a second, what does God's Word say about this?" You begin to change by first recognizing that it's an old, bad habit. There are so many attitudes you keep out of habit because you haven't recognized them or known that you could change them.

Many times your mate, your friends, or your children can help you with your "old thought" habits. Your children, especially, can be the best mirrors in which to see your "old" way of thinking. How do they talk, respond, and feel? Generally, you are the one who taught them, so they are a good picture of how you see yourself. Your mate or close friends may challenge the way you say things or your attitude with people. That's your chance to say, "Okay, I'm going to change my attitude. I'm going to act on the truth, and I'm going to do something about this." You can recognize the old habit and begin to change it.

Notice I said, "begin to change." It will not happen in one day. You are going to grow and change and work on yourself every day. You will not change everything all at once, but tomorrow you'll be better than today; and today, you're better than yesterday.

As you walk each day with the Holy Spirit, He is working in you to help you conform to the image of Christ. Remember Philippians 2:5, "Let this mind be in you which was also in Christ Jesus."

𝓑

BELIEVE THE BEST

Philippians 2:3

"*Let* nothing *be done* through selfish ambition or conceit, but in lowliness of mind let each esteem others better than himself."

God's best is that you do not talk badly or think badly about other people. There is no place for gossip in the life of a woman who wants to be happy and successful. You must be a person who thinks the best of other people.

What is gossip? Gossip is simply talking about another person with no intent to help them change. It is also talking badly about a person with no attempt on your part to change your thinking concerning the situation. There is a big difference between gossip and getting help for yourself with a situation that is bothering you. There may be times when you are "bugged" about something. Maybe you are angry or discouraged, and you may need to talk about it. It's fine to do that in order to get help for yourself, but you need to pick a person to talk to who will help you, not someone who will agree with you and get mad about the situation or at the other person.

Proverbs 18:8 says, "The words of a talebearer *are* as wounds, and they go down into the innermost parts of the belly." Gossip builds up a wall of distrust between people. By believing the worst of others, the very thing you want—friendship and acceptance—will be repelled from you. A person won't want to be close to you if they think you might gossip about them. When you talk negatively about someone to your mate or to a friend, it plants a seed of mistrust in them. In the back of their minds, they could wonder how you talk about them when they are not around.

Most humans (especially women) have to deal with wanting to know the "real" truth about a situation or person. How else is there so much to read on Facebook, Instagram, and Twitter about the "gossipy" things happening to people today? We seem to like to know the negative things that are going on in the world. That type of thinking allows you to think the worst rather than believe the best of others. There is always some truth to the things we read and hear. Not everything will be a lie, but if you are going to obey I Corinthians 13 and believe the best of all people, you need to stay away from those people and things that will cause you to get into gossip.

Fill up your time with good reports, listening to uplifting, inspiring stories, and your life will be so much fuller.

C

CONFIDENCE

Galatians 6:4

"But let each one examine his own work, and then he will
have rejoicing in himself alone, and not in another."

God has given each one of us different abilities and talents. He
loves to see you to develop your talents and use them for His
glory and to reach others. As you use your abilities, confidence
will develop within you. Successful people recognize they may
fail, but they will get up every time and try again. Einstein failed
many times. Edison failed over and over. But, in their eyes, each
failure brought them that much closer to success! Develop
confidence in yourself and see how God is working in you.

The first time I taught a Bible study, I didn't have the
confidence I have today. I failed many times, but I was

determined to try again. Gradually, my confidence grew, and I began to believe I was able to teach and help people.

Confidence seems to be built in a back-and-forth sway between blowing it and success, and from success to not quite hitting the mark. You go through life with times of success and times of failure, all the while growing. In the "downswings," you usually think, *That was the worst I have ever done.* Is that true?

Challenge yourself. If you are going for God and seeking Him, then you most certainly could not be at the lowest point. Living in Jesus and seeking His ways always brings growth. So, even though you may feel you are at your lowest point, you have reached way beyond the point when you did not have Jesus.

You must have confidence in yourself and rejoice in the work you have done. In the New King James Bible, Galatians 6:4 says, "But let each one examine his own work, and then he will have rejoicing in himself alone, and not in another."

Not everyone is supposed to do the same thing. You must do what God has called you to do. Too often you hear this message but go right on thinking your old ways. Shake yourself! You are the only you. Maybe you do not have the looks of a model. Does that model have your talents and personality? No! You may say, "Yeah, but I'd like to have her talents and personality." You will have to change that way of thinking. Quit beating your head against a brick wall and learn about your own styles, gifts, talents, and abilities. God must have wanted them on this earth. He gave them to you for a reason.

As you follow God's plan, you will develop confidence. You have been created exactly the way God wants you. You may have picked up a bad attitude that needs to change or a belief that might be a little off, but continue to press on. Know that we all must grow and change along the way. Have confidence in what you are doing. Have confidence in your decisions and don't compare them with other people's decisions and directions. Pick what you like and do it. Don't worry if someone else does it differently. It doesn't matter. You can be confident in what you do and feel good about the way you are doing it.

DECISIVE

Matthew 5:37

"But let your 'Yes' be 'Yes,' and your 'No,' 'No.' For whatever is more than these is from the evil one."

A fulfilled woman knows how to be decisive. She doesn't waver back and forth. She will say yes and no.

Indecision will cause you to make mistakes you would not make otherwise. A decisive person would not be swayed by, "Should I buy it now, or what if it goes on sale next week?" Ladies are especially prone to this way of thinking. By trying to get the "good" deals, we often pass up the best. You waste a lot of time thinking about what you could do instead of doing what you know to do.

When I learned how to say yes and no, I thought much more clearly. When you make decisions, you clear your mind. I have heard people who continually wonder:

Should I have a baby, should I not have a baby?

Should I get married, should I not get married?

Should I buy this house, should I not buy this house?

Should I exercise, should I not exercise?

Should I get up, should I stay in bed?

Should I go to the Bible Study, or should I stay home?

They don't seem to realize that if they made a decision, they would get their "bike" rolling. If their bike has no momentum, it can be super hard to steer. Once you start rolling, it is easier to steer in a new direction and to keep the bike moving. But, if you don't make a decision, every time the same situation comes up, you will think and wonder and have to decide what to do again. Why not make one decision?

Take exercise, for example. Why not just decide that you will exercise three to four times a week? Pick the kind of exercise you like, when you will exercise, and where you will exercise. That kind of decision will take away the, "Well, I don't know...maybe I'll do it next week."

If you are indecisive, though, you will go back and forth, not knowing what to do. You won't say yes and you won't say no. You won't say anything. You just think, *Hmmm, I don't know what to do.* Why not say yes or say no? Why not be honest? Be honest with who you are and what you want to do in each situation.

Sometimes making a decision is saying, "No, I do not want to have a baby." Just because everyone is doing it and everyone thinks you should, does not make it right for you. You can choose to think about your present decision again down the road, say in six months. Do not bring it up, or rehash it, or wonder about it again until the time you set for yourself. Live with your decision and be happy. It will bring about satisfaction and peace in your life. You will be much more confident and successful when you are a decisive person.

EXCITED

Psalms 21:1

"The king shall have joy in your strength, O LORD;

And in Your salvation how greatly shall he rejoice!"

King David was excited about God. He greatly rejoiced in the good things God had done and was doing for him. David is a great example for us. You can rejoice and be excited about life. When you are around someone who is excited about life, don't you want to stay around them? Don't you love to be with people who say, "I'm so excited! I like what I'm doing and I'm just having fun with life."? Then there's the other kind of person, the one who drags through life, barely alive. It's depressing to be in the same room with them. A fog seems to surround them.

Too often you get your eyes on little things that make you mad or irritated. Your husband may not say just the right thing,

28

the kids may not pick up things just right, or your mother may always be telling you the "right" way to do things. You seem to think on the not-so-perfect, the "I'm not measuring up," the "I wishes" instead of all the good, wonderful, happy things that are going on around you.

Be excited about life! There are new things happening every single day. Why get down? Maybe today wasn't the very best, but be excited you're alive. Be glad you can go to sleep, get up, and try again tomorrow. Look for what you can be glad about and forget the rest.

Stop right now!

Get a pen and paper and write down the reasons you have to rejoice. Write down at least ten things that are good in your life. Now think on these things. When things seem to be ho-hum and life in general is boring, stop and think on the ten reasons why you can rejoice and be excited about life. If you'll do it, people will be drawn to you like a magnet and success will be yours.

𝓕

FAITH

Hebrews 11:6

"But without faith *it is* impossible to please *Him,* for he who comes to God must believe that He is, and *that* He is a rewarder of those who diligently seek Him."

In order to be successful in life, you must have faith. Many times, "faith" has been a deep and difficult thing. My family has taught me more about faith than all the 900 faith sermons I've heard and taught through the years. Faith is simply believing.

If you look at your children and act like them, you would have the faith to move mountains. If I tell my granddaughter Willow I will take her swimming, she doesn't say, "But how are we going to get there?" And she doesn't worry if her swimsuit is dry or if I really can take her. She doesn't question, worry, fret, or scheme. She's ready to go! She says, "Okay, Grandma!"

That's how God wants you to act. When he says, "I'll fill you with my Spirit and my power," He wants you to say, "Okay, Dad."

Faith is no big, mystical thing. It is simply believing with childlike trust. To live as a successful woman, you need to have faith in God. When you are born again, you receive THE MEASURE OF FAITH, but what you do with your faith is up to you.

GOALS

Philippians 3:14

"I press toward the goal for the prize of the upward
call of God in Christ Jesus."

What are you pressing for? What do you want in your life? What do you want to do next week, next month, next year, five years from now? What are your mental, spiritual, financial, and social goals? Habakkuk 2:2 says, "Write the vision, and make it plain upon tablets, that he may run that readeth it." Write down your goals, dreams, and desires on paper. If you plan out what you want to do, you'll be amazed at how quickly it will be done.

Financially, you may want to do something within your home. How much money does it take to reach that goal?

Socially, what are your goals? Maybe you want to have more friends. How will you do it? You can make a plan to have a different couple over for dinner once a month. Or plan an activity with your family and another family, making the goal by the end of the year to have twelve different activities with twelve different families. That is one way to make a plan to have more friends.

What are your ministry goals? What are you doing to train yourself to minister effectively to people? You may say, "I believe God wants me to teach." What are you doing to learn how to teach? "I believe God wants me to work with computers." What are you doing to be able to work with computers?

Are you doing anything to reach your goals? You may say, "God told me to do it," but what is your plan of action? If you will obey the Word in Habakkuk 2:2, you will be well on your way to fulfilling the goals God has for you. But if you don't do anything to reach the goals you have now, you won't be prepared to move on to new and bigger goals in the future.

A few special thoughts: You mothers of young children may be thinking that this does not apply to you. You may think since you are home every day that having goals is no big deal. That thought is so untrue! You set the pace for your children, plus you have a strong influence on your mate. Reread this section on goals and go for it.

You mothers of grown children or almost grown children could be thinking, *I've never had goals before. I'm not really sure what to do.* Number one, you need to believe and then realize you have a lot of things in life yet to go after. God has much more for you to accomplish. Make a plan and then go for it. Jump into your new adventure.

Once you reach your present goals, you need to set new goals. Many of you will need to re-evaluate your goals from time to time. Check out what more you could do. Take the time to write down your goals for this week, this month, and this year.

In order to enjoy to the fullest what God has for you, you need to have visions and goals. There are two main reasons for this. The first is to help you find out what God has for you. By taking this time to plan, you will usually listen to God's leading. The second reason is so you can look back and see all that you've accomplished and see the mighty working of God in your life and how things have changed. Also, you will see all the unique ways God was able to help bring your vision to pass.

One last word: be realistic in setting your goals. Don't put down for your financial goals a one hundred percent increase. That's nearly impossible and will only discourage you. Be realistic, and then mix it with faith!

H

HELPFUL

Hebrews 10:24

"And let us consider one another in order to
stir up love and good works."

There is nothing more rewarding than the satisfaction that comes from helping another person. Does someone you know need encouragement? Can you pick up something and carry it across the room for someone? Can you give your neighbor a ride to the store?

Remember stories from years gone by when neighbors always helped each other? If someone had a problem, everyone for miles around gathered together to help. Do you think they didn't have anything else to do? They didn't have washing machines, microwave ovens, dishwashers, hair dryers, vacuum cleaners, or any of the other modern appliances we have today to help with their daily chores. I'm sure they were just as busy as we are today, yet they had been taught to help and trust people.

Let's rekindle the light of our forefathers and reach out with a helping hand. Consider other people. Say, "What can I do to help?" Not, "I'm so busy." We're all busy. It's easy to get very busy on this earth, yet we never seem to be too busy to do what we want to do.

The Word says to redeem the time and make the most of every opportunity. A fulfilled person thinks of other people. Are you willing to go out of your way when it is not convenient? Helping a family that has a member sick in the hospital isn't always convenient. Taking them a meal could interrupt your own dinner. Your family may need to eat at the same time. You could say, "I can't do it right now," but challenge yourself to go beyond how you feel and give all that you can to help another person.

In being a helpful person, don't forget about your own family. It's so easy to ask your kids to run upstairs for you or to tell your husband to get his own coffee. But being a truly helpful person must start at home. Be the one who is willing to help. Run upstairs when your kids need something or get up from your easy chair to get something for your husband. The best training for your family is to be a great example. Train yourself to be helpful and your family will follow in your footsteps.

I

INQUISITIVE

Luke 11:9

"So I say to you, ask, and it will be given to you; seek, and
you will find; knock, and it will be opened to you."

The word "inquisitive" reminds me of my grandkids, Willow and
Norah, who are always getting into anything and everything: the
flour, the refrigerator, then to the water, next on to the make-up
drawer. They love to explore. Children have so many questions.
They look, see, climb, and touch. Children want new things, they
go for things, they try things out, and they want to learn.

It seems that the older we get the more we think we know
everything, especially if you have been around Bible teaching for
any length of time. You can become very, very old instead of
being excited and searching. Too often you are not seeking. You

become apathetic and don't care about things. You aren't looking to find out what is new.

Scientists are children at heart, for they are always wanting to know more. They need to be inquisitive. They need to seek and ask questions about why it happened this way and not that way. You can be more like them. You can be more interested in finding "new" truth from the Bible.

Have you ever found something in the Word and you were so excited you told everyone? When was the last time you did that? Oh sure, you probably figured out later that they more than likely already knew your "new" revelation. Maybe you felt a little stupid for not already knowing what you shared. That doesn't matter. You discovered something good.

The Bible says, in Matthew 18:2, to be as a little child. Children are always learning and sharing what their parents already know. Does that stop them? Let's have a fresh outlook every day. Be in the "cruising stage," as they call it. The "cruising stage" is when young children get into everything. Nothing can be left out in sight or they will have it in their mouths within seconds. That is the way you should be with God's Word—inquisitive, wanting to know what it has to say.

You can become very religious and think, *Oh, I've already heard that. I know the Bible.* You may have heard the Scripture previously, but do you know it? Does faith come by having heard? Faith comes by hearing it, and hearing it, and hearing it.

The inquisitive person says, "I want to hear it again. What does I Peter 2:24 say? Hmmm, let me look at it again."

Recognize that you never know it. You always need to learn more. Sure, you're growing and maturing in the Word, but realize that you don't know it all. And that's okay.

J

JOYFUL

Psalms 5:11

"But let all those rejoice who put their trust in You;

Let them ever shout for joy, because You defend them;

Let those also who love Your name

Be joyful in You."

As you put your trust in God, you will rejoice. You do not need to wonder, be in fear, and worry whether or not you are going to make it. God is your defender. He is your guard.

Too often we try to take on the world all by ourselves. We say, "Bless God, I'm tough!" Why do something you do not have to? God's Word says to rejoice, recognizing that as we rejoice, we bring in the power and protection of God.

Psalms 16:11 says, "Thou wilt shew me the path of life: in thy presence is fullness of joy; at thy right hand there are pleasures for evermore." God will show us where to go and how to get there as we live with a spirit of rejoicing. You say, "Wendy, that seems impossible! I have three kids, two cats, and a husband who is a couch potato!" I guess God didn't mean you. Your situation is just too hard. No! Nothing is too difficult if we go for God's way.

How do I rejoice, you might ask? Here are some practical how-to's:

1. Think about good things that have happened to you. (You might have to go back a week or two.)

2. Share-talk with someone and tell them the good things happening in your life.

3. Thank God!

4. Sing, smile, laugh—do whatever you can to put a smile on your face. (Remember, the incident you are mad at today will more than likely be something to laugh about tomorrow.)

5. Become a person who sees the glass half full instead of half empty.

Philippians 4:4 says, "Rejoice in the Lord always: and again I say, Rejoice."

As happy, fulfilled women, let's remember to find things to be joyful about each day. As you do, you will find your life full of joy.

KINDNESS

Ephesians 4:32

"And be kind to one another, tenderhearted, forgiving one another, even as God in Christ forgave you."

"Tenderhearted" means being tender toward other people. Let's treat people the way you would treat a child: tenderly. Think about people. Don't push them around, but be thoughtful. A kind person is thoughtful and giving, thankful for other people. A kind person will give to and think about another person first.

Kindness doesn't just mean the tone of your voice is kind. Most people believe that someone who sounds very "sweet" is also very kind. That is not necessarily true. Many people may "sound" kind, but what do their actions show? Do they really think about others? Do their words build up or tear down?

Sweet-sounding people can say mean things. Kindness is an attitude of the heart, not an inflection in someone's voice.

Let me share a few specific examples of genuine kindness. You may have come home from a hard day at work, made a great dinner for your family, and were expecting help with cleanup. Suddenly, everyone has important things to do, which leaves you with the mess. You could get mad, scream, and deliver your "Nobody appreciates me" speech, or you could think kindly about your normally loving family and clean up with a good attitude.

What about that slow person driving in front of you? Do you yell, honk, and shake your fist at them? Or are you kind in thought and action? There are so many situations that come up daily to challenge us to be either kind or rough with people.

Check your heart, and if you haven't already, make the decision to be kind to people. When you are a kind person, you are also forgiving of others. You won't hold grudges toward people. Someone might have been rude and mean, and they might have done things that were uncalled for, but a kind person does not hold grudges. They will forgive and forget. They will believe the best of others.

I know it sounds easy when you read it in a book, but it's not always easy to live out. It can seem difficult, but that's when you call out for help. That's when you say, "God, not my will, but Yours be done."

And God is faithful. He will help you be the kind woman you desire to be.

L

LISTENER

James 1:19

"My dear brothers, take note of this: Everyone should be quick to listen, slow to speak and slow to become angry."

Don't we all want to be known as good listeners? I would rather talk to someone who is really listening to me than to someone who is thinking about what they are going to say next or someone thinking about other things. Have you ever been talking on the phone with someone who says "uh huh" in all the right places, but somehow you know you don't have their full attention? That can be pretty irritating.

Sometimes, maybe because of your own insecurity, you may have the habit of talking over the top of people. Many times it isn't that you don't want to listen, but because of your own insecurities, you talk and monopolize the conversation. Yikes!

So often in our relationships, especially marriage, listening gets lost in the shuffle. You assume things about each other and quit listening to what the other person has to say. Listening happens with the ear, but it also happens with the heart. A good listener will read between the lines and ask, "What is this person truly saying? What do they need?" A person who can "hear" and respond with love and kindness to the needs around them will be blessed in all they do. When you truly "hear" a person, you can help them.

A rule I diligently try to live by is to allow three seconds to pass before I respond to what a person has just said to me. Try it. I think you will be amazed how long three seconds lasts. It's not always easy, but you must close your mouth sometimes, listen with your ears, and more importantly, listen with your heart.

MUSICAL

Ephesians 5:19

"Speak to one another with psalms, hymns and spiritual songs.
Sing and make music in your heart to the Lord."

The Word says to be happy, singing and making melody in your heart to the Lord. When you sing, choose songs that are happy. Sing songs that are life-giving. The songs you sing (or don't sing) are a good indication of what's going on inside of you. If you're singing depressing songs or are not singing at all, question what you are thinking about. Perhaps you're worrying, fretting, or depressed, or wondering if people like you or not, if the bills will be paid, or if your kids are living for God the way you want them to. Sometimes we're so full of the cares of this world that we forget to sing happy songs to the Lord.

Once, when my son Caleb was small, he had a very high fever. Being a new mother, I was not familiar with this type of situation. As I held his listless little body and listened to his hurtful cry, I started to cry. I remember thinking, *This is not going to help me one bit,* but I had gotten myself so full of care over it that I didn't know what else to do.

Then I began to sing. When you hear yourself crying at the same time you're trying to sing, well, you have to start laughing. Once I laughed, it released me. I sensed my spirit rising up within me, and I said, "In the name of Jesus, devil, you get your hands off my son!" I sang and prayed, and Caleb fell sound asleep, later waking up strong and healthy.

God wants you to make a melody in your heart on a daily basis, not just when a disaster or a sad situation happen. You can download music on iTunes or Spotify that proclaim the Word and you can sing along. If you do, you will feel much better instead of feeling like a sluggard.

Sometimes you do not feel like being musical. You don't want to shout and sing and make a joyful noise unto the Lord. That's when you have the opportunity to work on your attitude and decide to do it anyway. Turn on music and allow it to uplift you. The day will fly by, and you will end your day with a smile on your face instead of a frown.

NEIGHBOR

Galatians 5:14

"The entire law is summed up in a single command:
'Love your neighbor as yourself.'"

We have been given a big command. God says we are to love people. Too often we make excuses like, "I love the people I know. And I always smile at the grocery clerk and wave at my neighbors. I really do love them!" That might sound good, but do you really want to reap the results of living the Word or do you want to live a mediocre, get-by lifestyle?

Loving people is actually easier than you may imagine. Loving is smiling at the clerk and waving at your neighbor when it's possible for you to do so. It also includes having people over to your home.

I am amazed at how few people will open up their homes and invite people in. We as believers could be the ones who regularly open up our homes for meals, Bible studies, and fellowship. Again, I can hear you say, "I don't have the time for that!" Proverbs 31 teaches us that the Virtuous Woman skillfully plans her days. We would all have an abundance of time to do the things we want to do if we planned what was important and cut out what was not important. Live your life according to the plans and priorities you have set for yourself, not according to the "emergencies" that can continually rob you of your time.

A good neighbor does more than have people over. A good neighbor smiles and talks to people whenever and wherever they can—in church, at school, on the job, or at the store. A neighbor is friendly and loves people. This attitude will cause you to go to people instead of thinking of ways to be too busy or how to get away from them.

You will be amazed at how much time you actually have and how full you will feel when you give of yourself and live neighborly.

O

OPTIMISTIC

Jeremiah 29:11

"For I know the plans I have for you," declares the LORD,
"plans to prosper you and not to harm you, plans to give
you hope and a future."

God is optimistic about you. Plan on being victorious in life. Plan on being optimistic, too. You must think as God thinks. He expects the best of you and for you. He is not looking for the worst. Did you read the Scripture at the beginning of this topic? I mean, really read it! God is thinking good thoughts about you. God doesn't agree with the negative things you've been thinking and saying about yourself. God sees your potential, not the problems you've been looking at.

You need to take God's thoughts and expect good things to come your way. Don't look for the negative, bad things and then say, "See, it always happens that way." Sometimes we have an "I told you so" attitude about the bad things in our lives. We confess out of our mouths the negative things we don't want to happen, and when we receive what we have believed, we wonder why God let it happen. If that's you, you can retrain yourself to expect the best. And if something happens that is not so good, learn to turn it around.

Have you ever heard the saying, "Look for the rainbow in the mud puddle"? You can be optimistic in any situation that comes your way.

Don't let the devil get you down. Look for the best in everything, and God will turn it around for your good.

℘

PEACEFUL

Philippians 4: 6, 7

"For I know the plans I have for you," declares the LORD, "plans to prosper you and not to harm you, plans to give you hope and a future, and the peace of God, which surpasses all understanding, will guard your hearts and minds through Christ Jesus."

Too often we get caught up in the cares of this life, like problems at the office, not having enough money for all our needs, society going downhill fast, having another fight with our mate, not liking who our kids hang around with, or worrying about the future. The list can go on and on. Unfortunately, the list perpetuates in our minds. That's why you must decide to be a person who lives at peace with God, with yourself, and with others.

Don't be the person who is always mad and frustrated, constantly stirred up and ready for a fight. If you develop the other attitudes that we have talked about, you will have an attitude of peace within yourself. These characteristics intertwine together, developing the personality of an overcoming person of God. It doesn't matter what your ministry is or what you do during the day, whether you are at home full-time or work outside the home. That really isn't the question. The question is what kind of person are you? What are you doing with the person you are? Are you going for your very best? Not your sister's best or your husband's best, but your best?

In going for the very best, you must develop peace within yourself. Allow the peace of God to rule in your heart, not what social media says or what another person does. You will never have peace until you decide you are in control of your own life. Then you can let the peace of God rule in your heart and mind.

Q

QUALITY PERSON

Colossians 3:23

"And whatever you do, do it heartily, as to
the Lord and not to men."

It is so easy to get "fuddy-duddy" and lazy with our lives. It seems as if some of the most popular TV shows are about overweight, lazy, undisciplined, sarcastic, rude people. It is so easy to act that way. Everyone seems to be able to relate, but does it really feel good inside? Does that undisciplined, lazy, sarcastic person lay her head down at night and thank God for such a happy, peaceful day? I strongly doubt it.

We never win when we do not act like Jesus. Sure, you may seem to win in a few situations by acting rude or sarcastic, but I'm talking about winning on the inside. I want to encourage you to not just get by in life. Invest yourself into the people, projects, work, ministry; whatever it is you are involved with.

Be a person who gives quality in all that you do. Don't allow mediocrity to come in and steal from you. When you praise God, give quality to Him. Praise Him with your whole heart, not just enough to get by with. When you spend time with your spouse and children, give to them heartily, which is what "quality" means. Give them all your attention. When you are with friends, give all you have when listening and sharing in having fun. The more you put into something, the more reward you will reap.

𝓡

RAINBOW PERSONALITY

A rainbow is refreshing, colorful, and shows forth the promises of God. It is a symbol of the destruction of the flood never coming on the earth again. When I see the rainbow, I have a feeling of security because I know God is there.

I love the beauty of a rainbow. As a Christian, that is the kind of attitude or vibe I want to give. I desire an attitude of freshness, beautiful color, harmony, and peace. In giving you the rainbow, God declared that He has kept no judgment against you. You need to have that same attitude toward people. When someone does you wrong, you may need to confront them, but don't hold a judgment against them and hold onto unforgiveness.

A famous pastor once told a story of a new believer, a woman who had been saved within the last six months. The woman said: "My family has been Godly and in the church for years. They are the best Christians in the whole town. They are beyond measure, always around, always doing everything that they should be doing. When they get sick, they always end up in the hospital and have operations. They always have things happening to them. On the other hand, my husband's family does not live for God. Sometimes they are faithful to live like Christians and sometimes they are not. But, when they get sick, they come to God, and they ask God to heal them and He does. I can't understand that."

The pastor said, "I can tell you one thing. Your family is not quick to forgive."

The lady's mouth dropped open. "You're right. They save it up for a long time."

He asked, "But they will forgive, won't they?"

"Yes, they have to forgive because it is in the Bible," she replied.

Then the pastor said, "Your husband's family is quick to forgive."

The woman answered, "If my mother-in-law even thinks she offended someone or if there was any problem in a situation, she takes full credit and asks for forgiveness immediately. She is quick to ask for forgiveness, and so is everyone in their family."

"Yes, they hold no judgment in them," the pastor said. "Your family, they hold madness, but they forgive because they have to. That won't bring the healing power of God in their bodies because they only do it because of religious duty, not because of a heart change."

If you want to be a healthy, strong person, develop an attitude that is quick to forgive. Be a person who holds no judgment against another. Allow God's rainbow personality to shine forth in your life. Quick forgiveness brings quick peace.

S

SERVANT

Philippians 2:3-5

"*Let* nothing *be done* through selfish ambition or conceit, but in lowliness of mind let each esteem others better than himself. Let each of you look out not only for his own interests, but also for the interests of others. Let this mind be in you which was also in Christ Jesus."

Notice that you are to have the same way of thinking that Jesus had. HE IS KING OF KINGS AND LORD OF LORDS. He is the One that saved us from going to Hell. He came and esteemed us better than Himself. He made Himself a servant to us. Our Leader, our King, the One with control over the whole universe said, "I'll be your servant." He humbled Himself and gave of Himself to people.

Yet our worldly standards say it is not ideal to be a servant. They don't know what it really means to truly serve. The word "servant" has the connotation of being a low-life, someone under your feet, not as good. In the church, we all say we want to be the servants, but many times in our hearts that is not true. We want to make sure we are recognized to be just as important as someone else. Often, because we don't have a true servant's attitude, we will be in competition with people around us. We want to gain a certain level of authority.

We don't like to admit it or even think about it, but the attitude from the world has gotten into many of us. We watch TV, engage with social media, talk to people, and are socialized to believe that servants are not as good as leaders. We've been told that the leader is the important person and the servant is the dummy that never stands up for their point of view. THAT IS NOT TRUE.

Anyone who is a good leader must be a good servant. That worldly way of thinking will only cause competition and bad feelings. Remember what Philippians 2:3 said? "Let nothing be done through strife and vainglory, but in lowliness of mind let each esteem the other better than themselves."

Working as a team is a great way to understand being a servant. It will eliminate the competition that we can get so involved in. Working as a team will also bring about a true servant's attitude in each of the teammates. We need to work together and serve one another if we want to succeed and win more people on to the team.

Each team member must play their position, do their best, and know exactly what to do to defend their team members. It takes time, practice, and discipline to be the best for their position on the team.

This is so true of the Body of Christ. Each of us has been given a place by God to use our gifts and talents. Yet, too often we are trying to play another position instead of growing, learning, and developing our own spot on the team. Let's learn to love our position so we can protect the rest of the team and have fun in life instead of trying to be someone we are not.

T

TRUTHFUL

Ephesians 4:25

"Therefore, putting away lying, *"Let each one of you speak truth with his neighbor,"* for we are members of one another."

"Be a truthful person…no way!" "I won't feel safe." "People won't like me." "A little white lie never hurt anybody." Haven't we all thought at least one of these at some time in our life? Not only thought that way but acted that way?

I used to sell shoes, and on a regular basis, women would say, "I'll hide these shoes away for a week or so and my husband will never know I bought them. What he doesn't know won't hurt him." It seems that one statement is what most soap operas are made of. Lie, lie, lie! Cheat and get away with whatever you can. Hide anything from your past, hide anything in your thoughts that a person could use against you.

Is this God's way of thinking? John 8:32 says, "And ye shall know the truth, and the truth shall make you free." The truth will make you free. Hmmm, that doesn't sound like what TV folks say. Some of us have been taught that the truth hurts and causes pain so never get close to the truth.

Jesus said in John 14:6, "I am the way, the truth, and the life; no man cometh unto the Father, but by me." That sounds a lot different than "the truth hurts."

God has given us the message of truth to live in. One of the worst bondages to live with is holding onto a secret from your past or lying about how you think or feel. God wants you to be free from your past. When there are no secrets and everything is out in the open, you can expect to live in forgiveness. When you let your spouse and your friends know some of your unrenewed thoughts, they can love you and help you overcome. But if you try to hide them, you do not allow God's people to help you to overcome, and that will cause you to live alone, like an island. That's a very painful way to live.

Be truthful with yourself, your spouse, your friends, and your family. When you are honest, you will allow yourself to live in peace and forgiveness.

$\mathcal{U}$

UNDERSTANDING

Galatians 6:1

"Brethren, if a man is overtaken in any trespass, you who *are* spiritual restore such a one in a spirit of gentleness, considering yourself lest you also be tempted."

We who are Christians have the understanding and inner strength to give of ourselves to help those involved in problems. Remember what I shared about believing the best of all people and not getting involved with gossip? It is easy to jump in on gossip.

The Word says, "You who are spiritual restore them LEST YOU ALSO FALL." Women seem to be the worst for loving gossip. You say, "Wendy, I'm a Christian." So am I, but that doesn't make us exempt. We have to get a hold of ourselves and be careful not to hear and pass on "ear tickling" reports. Gossip is passing on a report that would hurt another person, with no intent to go to the person to see if it is true or not.

It's important to realize that when you gossip and enjoy hearing about those who are in sin, you open yourself up for that SIN TO ATTACH ITSELF TO YOU. It is foolish to get excitement or satisfaction from another person's problems.

Proverbs says that when a person falls into calamity, be careful that you don't laugh or that calamity will come on you. Never have an attitude of smugness or satisfaction when a person is going through a tough situation. We who are spiritual are to pray. If you can minister and help meet that person's need, do it. Be an understanding person, not judgmental. Support people and help them succeed.

VISION

Proverbs 29:18

"Where *there is* no revelation, the people cast off restraint; But happy *is* he who keeps the law."

What is your vision for life? Your vision has to do with your dreams, your goals, and your hopes. Where there are no dreams, goals, and hopes, people perish. What do you want to do with your life? Do you want to simply get by? If you don't have a vision for more than just surviving, that is all you are going to get.

How successful would you be if you didn't care what was happening in different areas of your life? Do you know the kind of parent you want to be? Have you envisioned yourself as the prime educator of your children? As their spiritual leader? As the P.E. director in your home? Do you have a vision of successfully managing your career? Do you see yourself getting promotions? Do you even think beyond what is happening today? Find out what it is you want to accomplish and keep that vision in front of you.

Someone once told me, "When we started coming to the church my biggest vision was that I wanted to be a Prayer Partner, and I just believed I could accomplish that goal. I worked at developing myself so I wasn't so afraid." She believed the Word and studied the Word about overcoming fear and then she signed up for the Prayer Partner's class. She went through the class three times in order to plant the vision within her. Once she got the training, she acted on her vision. The first time she went forward in an altar call and stood behind a person, her legs and knees were shaking. She said when that woman turned around and shook her hand, fear left her. Just like that! Her vision was complete.

She realized then that she needed a new vision. Her new vision was to work in the prison ministry. She is now developing herself to be able to reach that vision.

Do you have a vision, desire, or direction? What are your goals? What are you doing to reach your goals?

Some practical areas that you can set goals for are:

1. Personal: spiritual, physical, social;
2. Business: how much increase this year in business, in money;

3. Family: goals with your mate, with your children, family vacations; and

4. Financial: increase in your tithe, increase in your salary.

This is a simple outline. Of course, you can be much more specific.

Successful people keep a vision in front of them and take action to reach their vision.

WORSHIP

John 4:23

"But the hour is coming, and now is, when the true
worshipers will worship the Father in spirit and truth;
for the Father is seeking such to worship Him."

What is worship? Is it bowing down, closing your eyes, or lifting
your hands? Is it folding your hands, singing a song, or sitting
quietly? It is all of this, and even more.

Worship is more than acting a certain way or saying the right
words. Worship is an attitude of your heart, one of honor,
respect, love, praise, and excitement.

Psalms 103:1 says, "Bless the Lord, O my soul: and all that is
within me, bless his Holy name." We have the privilege and
opportunity to love God all the time. We worship Him and bless
His name by our act of worship in giving: financially, physically,

socially, and spiritually. We worship God when we are obedient to His Word. When we do what the Bible says.

A few examples of these are:

1. Being a joyful giver;
2. Encouraging fellow believers;
3. Hiding His Word in our hearts;
4. Keeping our bodies healthy and strong, as His temple; and
5. Singing and lifting our hands.

These are all good examples of worshipping God. God wants more than lip service. He wants our hearts to follow after Him! He wants us to bless Him with all of us, not fifty percent.

X-RAY PERSON

Luke 12:2

"For there is nothing covered that will not be revealed,
nor hidden that will not be know."

Successful Christians are to live openly and honestly before God and man. We need to realize that God knows our thoughts and the intents of our hearts. He knows the way we live at home where no one else sees us, and He sees all the things we try to hide. But He says, "Hey, it's going to be revealed anyway. Why not admit your faults and get the help you need to change it." God doesn't want us to have to slip around and hide ourselves. He wants us to be open and free. That openness will bring about a tremendous healing in our lives.

Let's allow our Christian brothers and sisters to "X-ray" us by being honest and then we can get a diagnosis from the Word and be healed.

γ

YOUNG

A fulfilled person is someone who is young at heart. Someone who is willing to do new things and try new ideas. In order to succeed in life, we need to be open and ready for new things. A young person is ready to try anything. They have the attitude that says "Go for it!" They don't say, "We've always done it this way, and that's the way it's going to be!"

As you get older, it can be so easy to not truly hear those who are younger. You may have already done that, had that thought, or tried that idea. History has proven over and over how much age can and cannot matter.

If you decide you are old, you are. Most likely, life and all the newness it can bring is now old and boring, bringing you aches and pains. Yet if you decide to live full-on, with your eyes open wide in wonder, it is amazing what you will see. You will witness that the color of life is real and alive. Do not live by your earthly age, rather live with your eye on the prize and with the joy of life!

Z

ZEALOUS

Titus 2:14

"Who gave Himself for us, that He might redeem us from every lawless deed and purify for Himself *His* own special people, zealous for good works."

Jesus gave Himself for us so that we could be doing good works. Not because we have to, but because we love God so much that we want to. Because we're so excited about what He has done for us, we can't wait to tell others so He can help them, too. Let's go for it, be zealous and sold out for God. Feel good about what you are doing.

God wants us "red-hot" for good works. The world thinks nothing of yelling and jumping and getting excited about a football game. But let a Christian get excited about worshipping God, and they start saying we are peculiar. That's right!

God said it in Titus. He says we are to be peculiar, and the way people will know it is if we're zealous in doing our good works. Let's be sold out for God, letting our lights shine before men. And then we will achieve true success. Our Father will say to us, "Well done, thou good and faithful servant."

About the Author

Wendy Treat is an ordained minister and pastors with her husband, Casey, at Christian Faith in Seattle, Washington. Wendy is a powerful Bible teacher and an anointed leader in the body of Christ. She ministers weekly to the women of Christian Faith and appears regularly on Casey's weekly television broadcast. She is committed to helping all people live the abundant life God has provided.

Books by Wendy Treat:

Shoes Wisely
Positive Childbirth: God's Plan
Woman! Get in Your Place

For more information on other product by
Wendy Treat, please write to:

Wendy Treat
P.O. Box 98800
Seattle, WA 98198

Made in the USA
Columbia, SC
20 May 2019